C

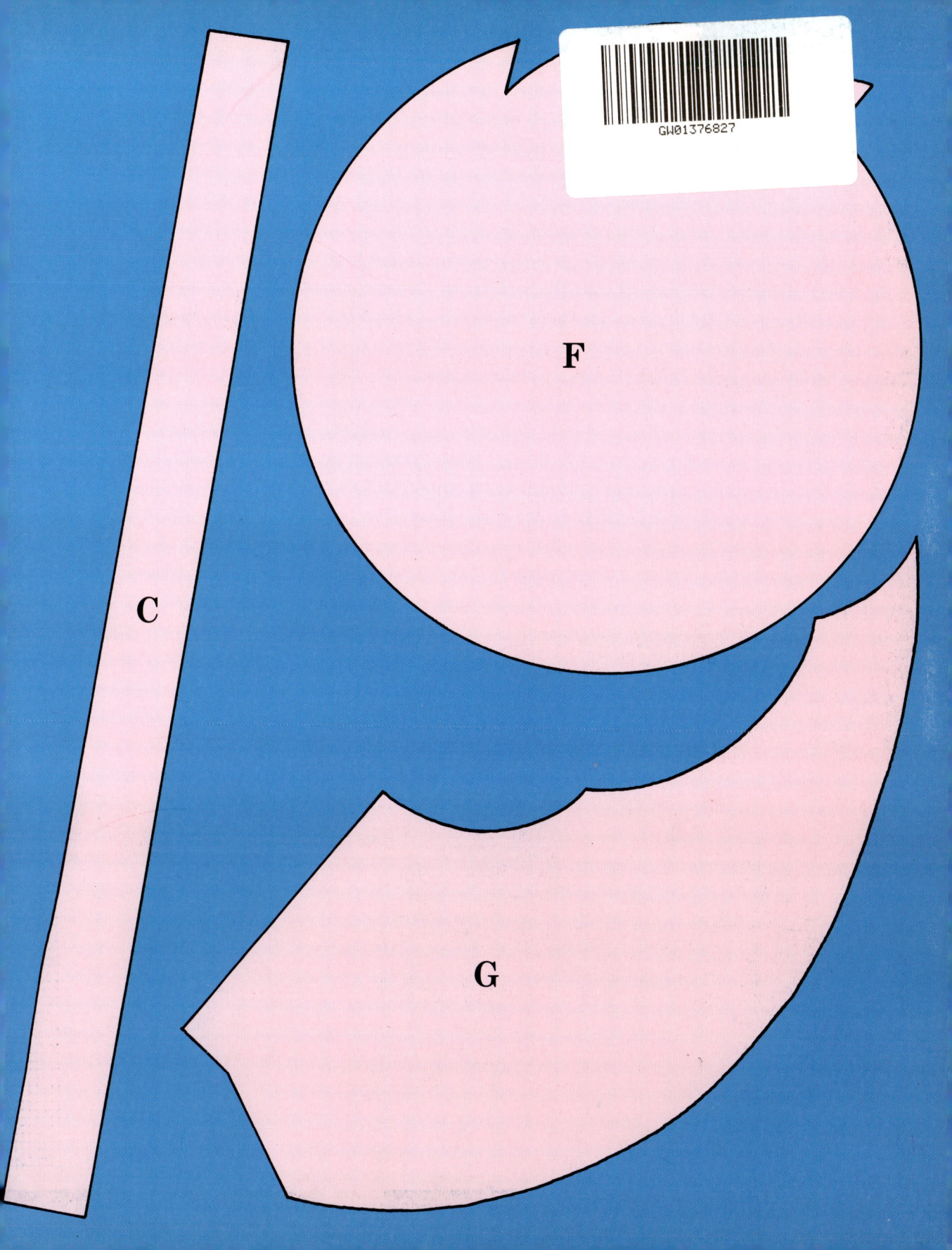

F

G

LEVERS

MAKE IT MOVE

Wendy Arnold-Dean

Photographs by Chris Fairclough

Belitha Press

First published in Great Britain in 1993 by
Belitha Press Limited
31 Newington Green, London N16 9PU

Copyright © Belitha Press Limited 1993

Illustrations/photographs copyright © in this format by Belitha Press Limited 1993
All rights reserved. No part of this book may be reproduced or utilised in any form or by any means, electronic or mechanical, including photocopying, recording or by any information storage and retrieval system, without permission in writing from the Publisher.

ISBN 1 85561 171 6
Typeset by Goodfellow & Egan Ltd, Cambridge
Printed in China for Imago

British Library Cataloguing in Publication data for this book is available from the British Library

Acknowledgements
Thank you to
Canonbury Book & Toyshop, Upper Street, London N1
for loan of mobile (p 31)
Invicta Plastics Ltd, Harborough Rd, Oadby, Leicester LE2 4LB
for loan of bucket scales (p 6 and 21)
and to our models, Sophie, Rachel and Sam

Editor: Rachel Cooke
Designer: Jane Felstead
Diagrams: Eugene Fleury
Puppets: Deborah Crow

CONTENTS

What is a lever?	4
Why are levers so useful?	6
Bits and pieces	10
1: Head and tail	12
2: Legs	14
3: The body	16
Linking levers	18
4: Support	20
5: Wings	22
6: Flapping	24
7: Ready for take off	26
Variations	28
Levers all around us	30
Glossary and index	32

What is a lever?

A **lever** is a simple **tool** that helps us move things. It is a bar or rod that swings, or **pivots**, about a fixed point. If the part of the bar on one side of the fixed point is moved, the other side moves as well. Only the fixed point stays in the same place. It is the way a see-saw moves.

Some levers have a fixed point at one end of the bar. This type of lever swings in the way a door does on its hinge.

The push or pull that moves the lever is called the **effort**. The thing or part being moved is called the **load**. The fixed point is called the **fulcrum**.

Effort

Fulcrum

Load

Levers are all around us. We use levers all the time, although we may not always know it. There are a few examples on this page. They are part of our everyday lives. This book shows you why levers are so useful.

You can also find out for yourself just how levers work, by making your own moving dragon puppet. It flaps its wings and nods its head. You move it by using levers.

Why are levers so useful?

Levers can be used to balance different things.

For two different things to balance exactly, they must weigh the same. If you know the weight of one thing, you can use a lever to find out the weight of another.

Some levers can help you to move something you cannot reach with your hands.

When you use a lever, it can turn a small movement you make into a bigger one or it can turn your big movement into a smaller one.

When you use a hammer to knock in a nail, its head moves much further than your hands. Pull the nail out and your hands move a long way but the hammer's head moves only a short way.

Levers can move something in the opposite direction to the way you push or pull.

Most useful of all, levers can help to make better use of your strength or power so that you can do things that would normally be very difficult or even impossible.

When using a lever, if you move a longer distance than the object you are moving, your push or pull is given extra force.
Using wire cutters, your hand moves further than the blades. This gives added strength so the blades cut easily through the wire.

If you move a shorter distance than the object you are moving, then you may have to push or pull the lever harder but the object will move further. Think of waving a big flag. Your arms don't move as far as the flag but you have to work hard to get it really flying.

Bits and pieces

The shapes on these pages are the ones you will need to make your dragon puppet. You will find these shapes drawn full-size at the front and back of the book. Trace them onto thin paper and cut the shapes out. You can use these paper shapes to draw round on the card you use to make your puppet.

If you don't want to use these shapes, you can always make up your own.

You will need

thin paper
a pencil
scissors
strong card
a ruler
a single-hole hole puncher
paper fasteners
a garden or dowel stick
sticky tape
coloured pens and paper for decoration

11

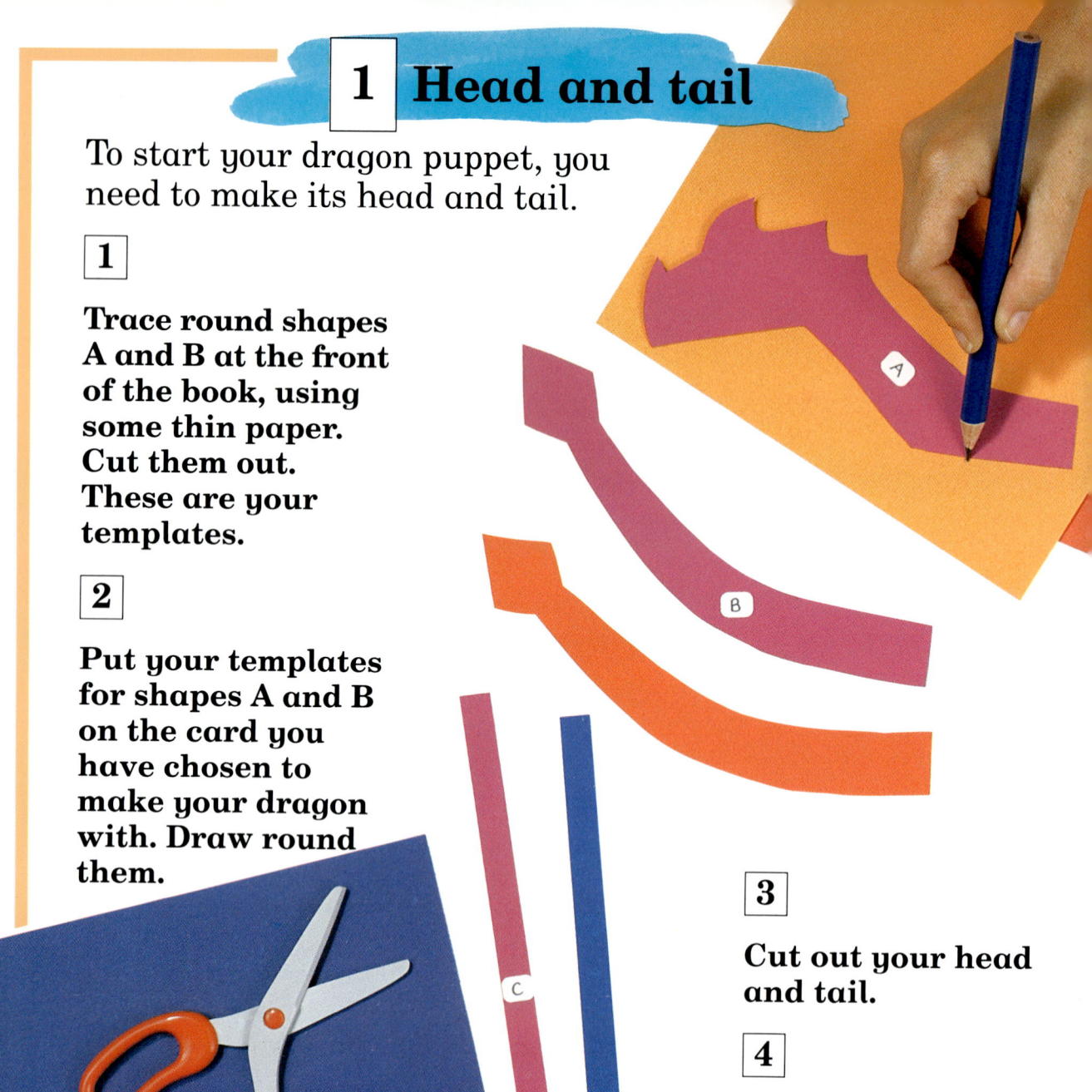

1 Head and tail

To start your dragon puppet, you need to make its head and tail.

1

Trace round shapes A and B at the front of the book, using some thin paper. Cut them out. These are your templates.

2

Put your templates for shapes A and B on the card you have chosen to make your dragon with. Draw round them.

3

Cut out your head and tail.

4

Using a ruler to give a straight edge, make a paper template for shape C. Draw round it on the card and then cut the shape out.

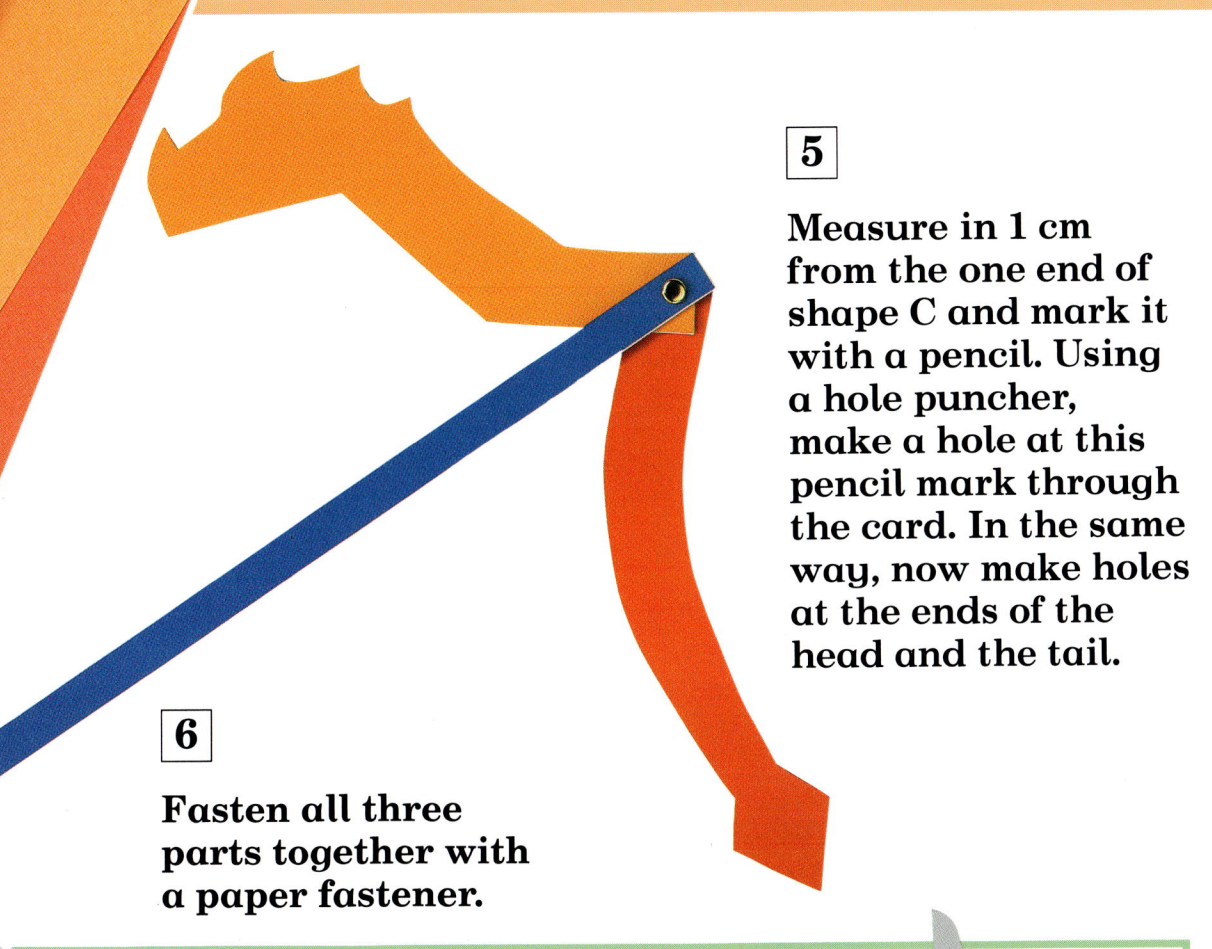

5

Measure in 1 cm from the one end of shape C and mark it with a pencil. Using a hole puncher, make a hole at this pencil mark through the card. In the same way, now make holes at the ends of the head and the tail.

6

Fasten all three parts together with a paper fastener.

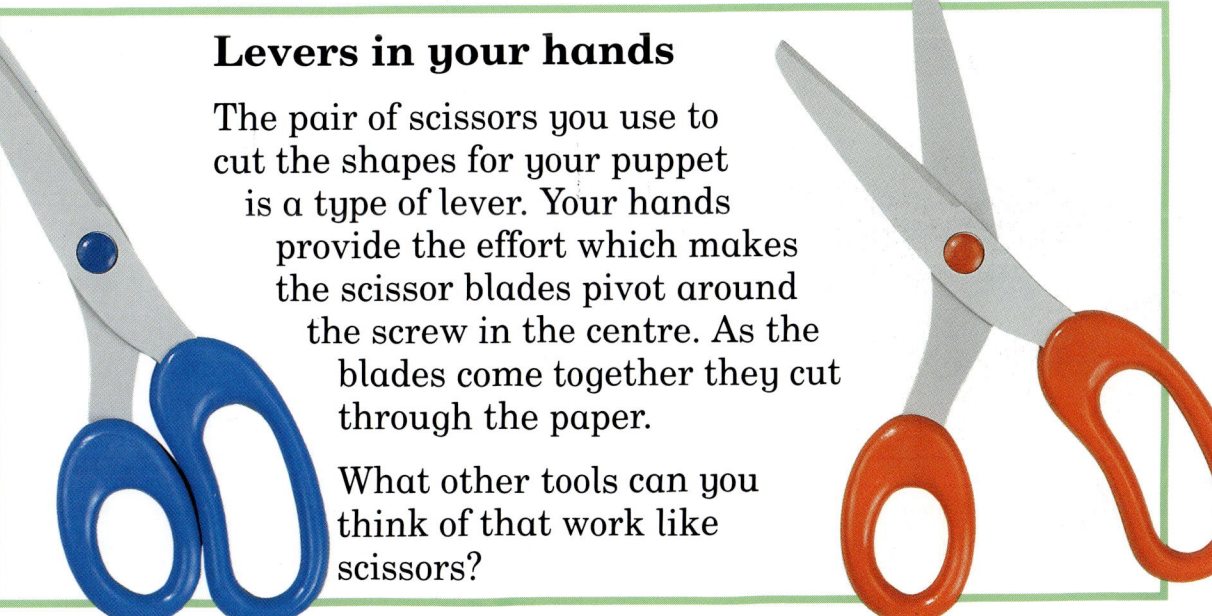

Levers in your hands

The pair of scissors you use to cut the shapes for your puppet is a type of lever. Your hands provide the effort which makes the scissor blades pivot around the screw in the centre. As the blades come together they cut through the paper.

What other tools can you think of that work like scissors?

2 Legs

Next you add legs to your puppet.

1

Make paper templates for shapes D and E. Use these to draw the leg shapes on card. Cut out one of each shape.

2

Make a hole 1 cm from the top end of the leg.

3

Take the centre strip (shape C) and measure 5 cm from the paper fastener down its centre. Mark this with a pencil. Make a hole with the hole puncher at this mark.

4

Fasten the legs to the centre strip to shape C with a paper fastener at the new hole.

5

Make a second hole in the head, tail and legs 4 cm from the paper fasteners.

The effort to move a load

The force, usually a push or pull, that moves a lever is called the **effort**. When we use a lever, we usually provide the effort. We have to push or pull one part of the lever to make another part move. This other part, and anything that moves with it, is called the **load**.

Sometimes the load is easy to spot.

Sometimes it is simply part of the lever itself.

When you have finished your puppet, its head, tail and legs will be levers and part of them will be the load. Your hand pushing and pulling on the centre strip will provide the effort to move them.

3 The body

Your dragon has got a head, a tail and some legs. Now it needs a body.

1

First draw the body shape on the card, using a paper template of shape F. Cut out the body.

2

Lay the head, tail and legs over the body. They should lie straight across the centre strip, with the paper fasteners down the middle of the body. Mark the body with a pencil through the extra holes you made.

3

Using a hole puncher, make holes through the body at these pencil marks.

4

Join the head, tail and legs to the body with paper fasteners through these holes.

Fixed points

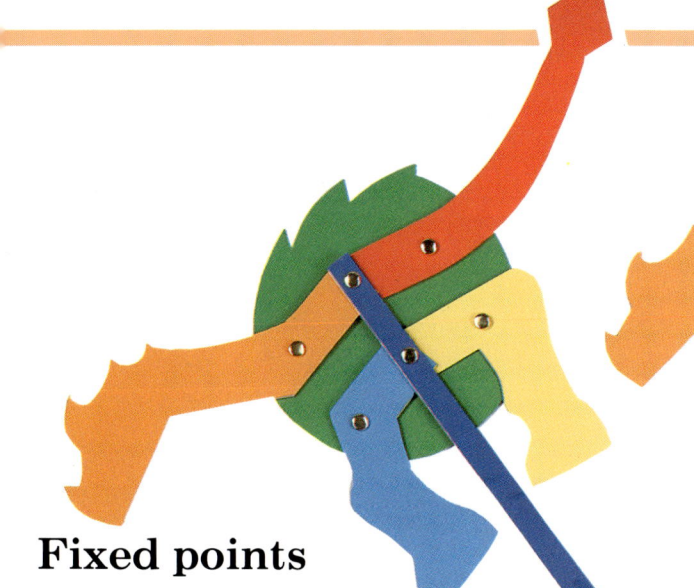

Now you can see that the head, tail and legs on your puppet are levers. Holding the body, move the centre strip up and down. The limbs pivot about the paper fasteners which attach them to the body.

These paper fasteners are the fixed points of the levers. They are called the **fulcra**. One of them on its own is called a **fulcrum**.

Where do you think the fulcrum is on each of these objects?

17

Linking levers

If two or more levers are joined together this is called a **linkage**.

Your dragon puppet has now got four levers joined together by the centre strip. You have made a linkage. Now you only have to push and pull the centre strip for all four levers to move.

Linkages are found in many different machines. They can be very useful. They can be used to make some simple machines.

18

The linkages in some machines are much more complicated. For example, a piano works by a series of linked levers.

Where do you think the levers are joined on the machines shown on these two pages?

19

4 Support

To hold your puppet properly, you need a support stick.

1

Lay the garden or dowel stick down the centre of the body's back, about 2 to 3 cm from its top. Make sure the bottom of the stick lies below the bottom of the centre strip.

2

Tape the stick firmly onto the back of the body. Be careful not to cover any of the paper fasteners as they need to be able to move freely.

3

Now you don't need to hold your puppet's body to move it. Hold the stick with one hand and pull the centre strip with the other.

Types of lever

There are three kinds of lever. They are called **first class levers**, **second class levers** and **third class levers**. This does not mean that some are better than others but they are just different.

First class levers

A **first class lever** is one where the fulcrum is in the middle, in between the effort and the load. The head, tail and legs of your puppet are all first class levers.

Here are some more examples of first class levers.

5 Wings

Most dragons have wings so now you can make some for yours.

1

Make a paper template of shape G and use it to cut out two wing shapes. Ask an adult to help you make a fold line 1 cm in from the inside edge of each wing by scoring the card with a sharp edge.

2

Tape one wing onto the front of the body above the paper fasteners and centre strip. Take care not to tape across the moving parts.

3

Turn the puppet over and tape the other wing onto the back of the body level with the first one.

4

Fold down each wing along the score lines you made.

Second class levers

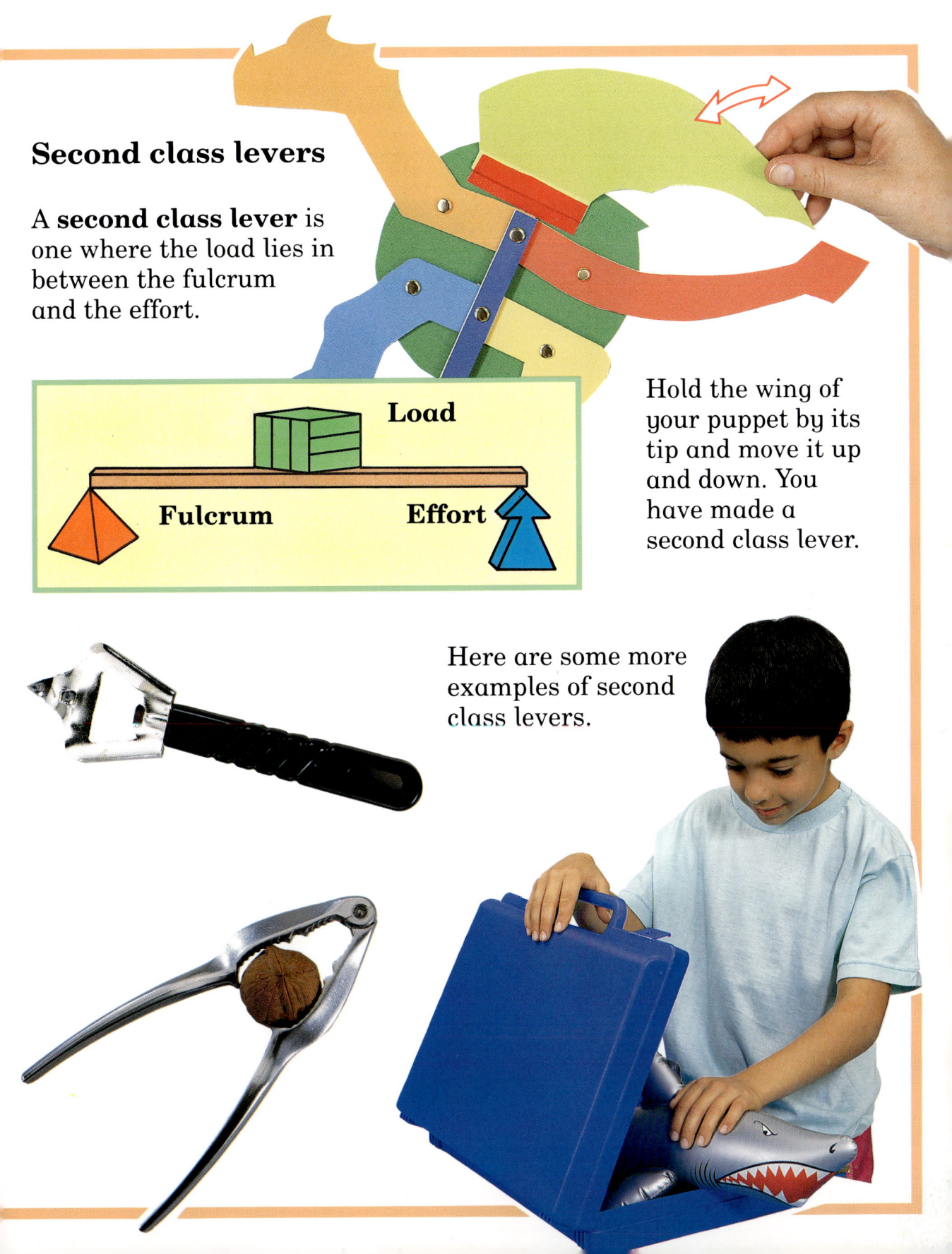

A **second class lever** is one where the load lies in between the fulcrum and the effort.

Hold the wing of your puppet by its tip and move it up and down. You have made a second class lever.

Load
Fulcrum
Effort

Here are some more examples of second class levers.

6 Flapping

Now you need to add control strips to your dragon's wings so that you can move them at the same time as its other limbs.

1

Use your template for shape C to cut out two more shapes from card. Cut 2 cm off the end of each piece to make it shorter than the centre strip. Ask an adult to help you make fold lines 3 cm in from the top end of each strip.

2

Tape the fold end of each strip to the middle of the underside of each wing.

3

Fold each strip along its fold line so that it hangs down beside the centre strip.

Third class levers

A **third class lever** is one where the effort is made in the middle of the lever, in between the fulcrum and the load.

Rather than moving a wing by holding its tip in your hand as you did on page 23, now move it by its wing strip. The effort which moves the wing is in its centre. By adding a wing strip, you have made the wing into a third class lever.

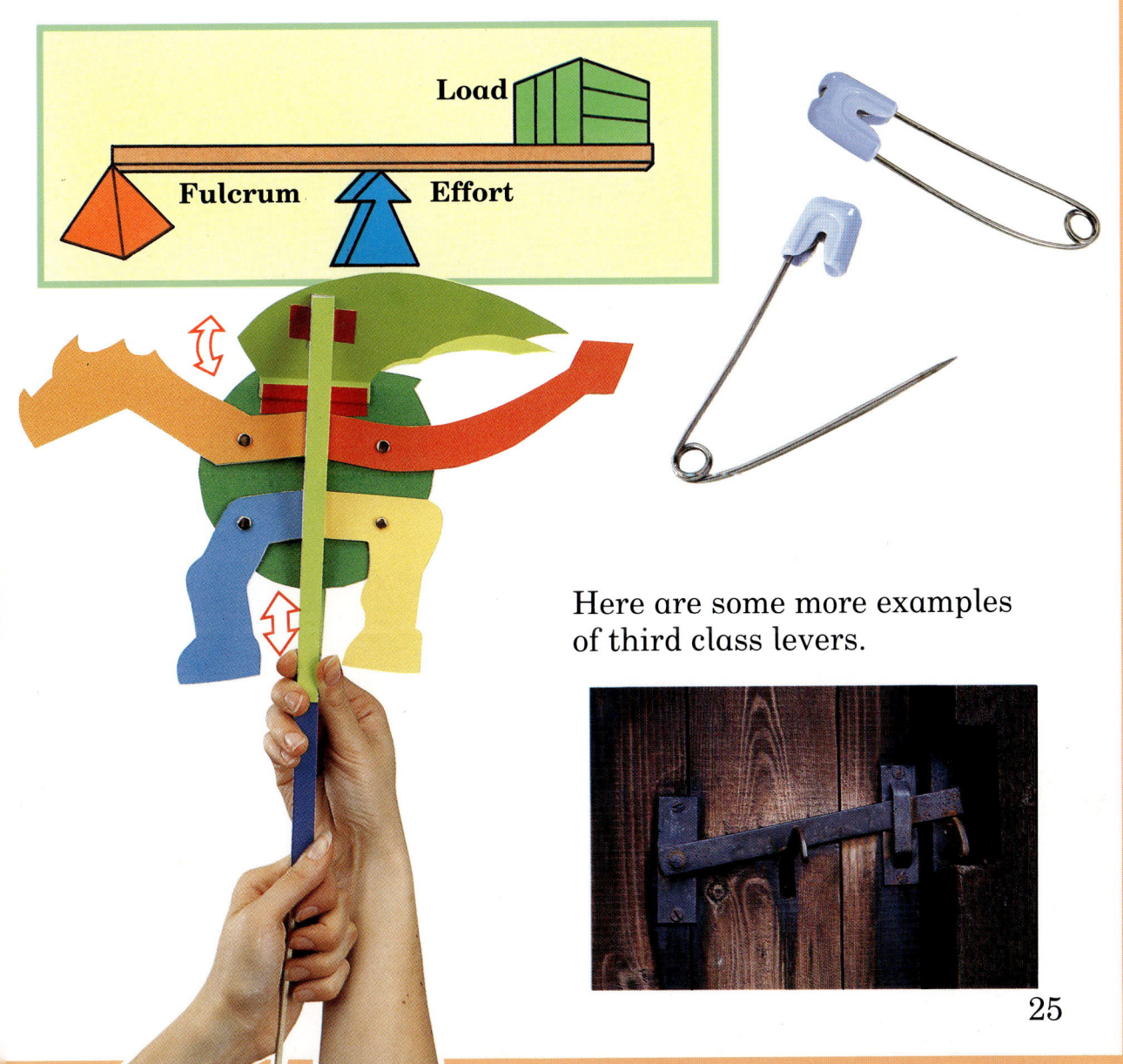

Here are some more examples of third class levers.

25

7 Ready for take off

1

Cut out a small strip of card. It should be about 1 cm wide and long enough to fit loosely around the three control strips of your puppet. Loop this card into a circle and tape its ends together.

2

Slip the circle around the handle of your puppet and tape it to the two wing strips.

Your puppet is now ready for take off.

Hold the stick with one hand. If you pull the card loop, the wings will move.

Pull the centre strip and the head, tail and legs will move.

26

Pull the loop and strip together and everything will move! Now your dragon can fly or walk away!

Body levers

Animals with skeletons – which include people – really do use levers to move. Their bones are the levers, the joint where two bones meet is a fulcrum and their muscles provide the effort.

Variations

Now your puppet is finished you can decorate it. Try drawing a face on it or sticking on some coloured card or sequins.

Why not try designing and making some different puppets that move by using levers? There are some ideas on these two pages.

29

Levers all around us

It's not just puppets that move by levers. Lots of other toys do as well and many different machines. Here are just a few examples. What other machines can you think of that use levers?

31

Glossary

These are some useful words you may need when talking about levers. They are shown in darker type when they first appear in the book or when they are explained.

Effort: the force, often a push or a pull, that is used to work a lever. When we use a lever, we usually provide the effort.

Fulcrum (fulcra): when using a lever, the fulcrum is the only part of it which does not move. It is the fixed point about which the lever turns or *pivots*. We use the word fulcra to mean more than one fulcrum.

Lever: a bar or rod that swings or turns about a fixed point. Levers are simple machines which we use to help us move things. There are three different types of lever:
   First class lever: a lever where the *fulcrum* is in between the *effort* and the *load*.
   Second class lever: a lever where the *load* is in between the *fulcrum* and the *effort*.

Third class lever: a lever where the *effort* is in between the *load* and the *fulcrum*.

Linkage: two or more *levers* joined together.

Load: the object that is being moved when using a *lever*. The load is sometimes big and heavy and easy to see. But sometimes the load is part of the lever which makes it harder to spot.

Pivot: to turn or swing about a fixed point. A *lever* pivots around its *fulcrum*. The word pivot is also sometimes used instead of the word *fulcrum*.

Tool: a simple machine or implement which helps us to do a task more easily or better than we would be able to on our own. A *lever* is a type of tool.

Index

effort 4, 13, 15, 21, 23, 25, 27
fixed point *see* fulcrum
fulcrum 4, 17, 21, 23, 25, 27
levers, all around us 4, 30-31
levers, body 27
levers, linking 18-19
levers, types of 21-24
   first class 21
   second class 21, 23
   third class 21, 25
levers, uses 6-9, 13
linkage 18-19
load 4, 15, 21, 23, 25
puppet, making 12-17, 20-27
puppet, variations 28-29
tools 4, 13

A

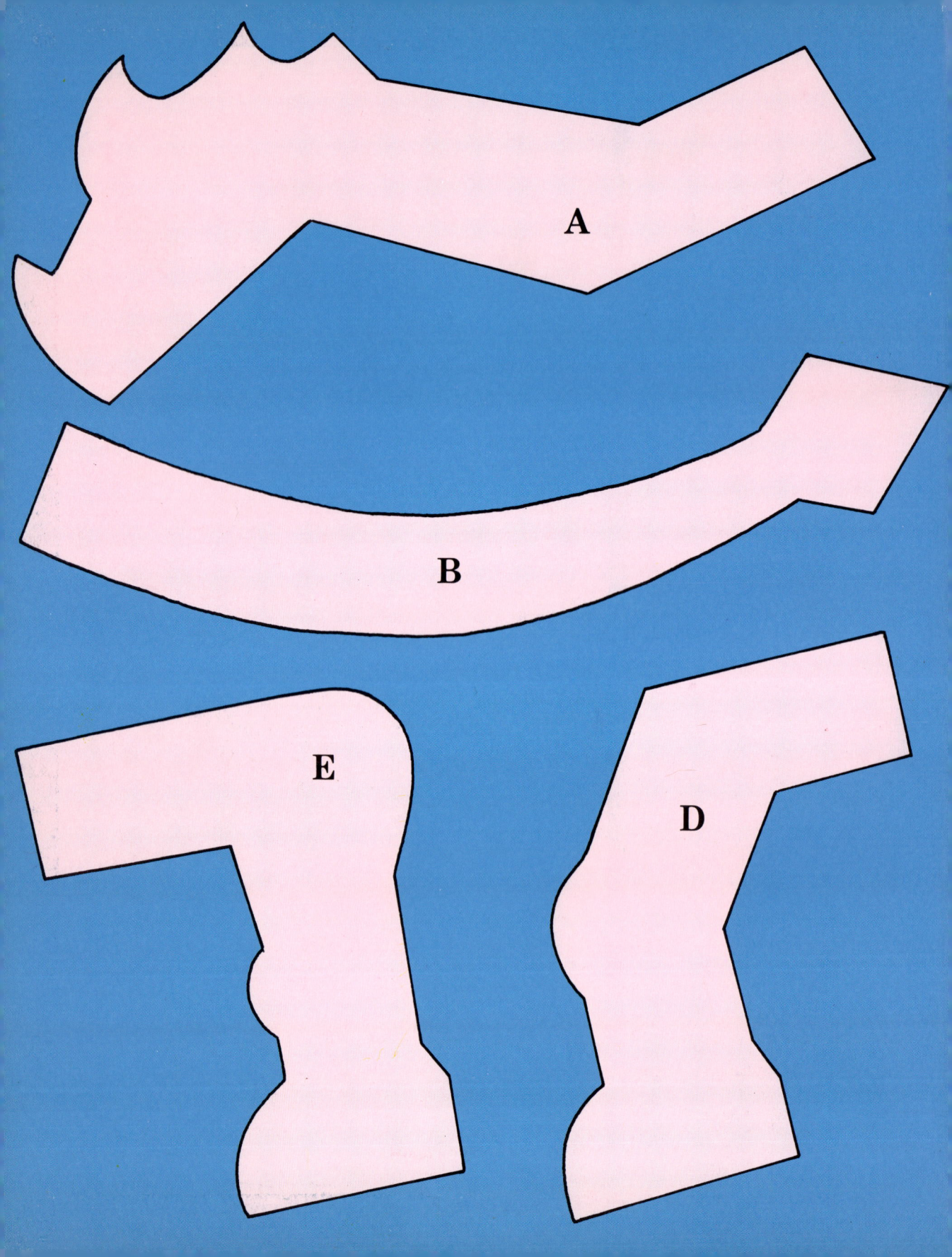

B

E   D